A Children's Fully Illustrated Book of Poetry

DAVID AND GOLIATH

Plus Fifteen Other Favorite Bible Stories

DWAIN FOWLER

LifeRich Publishing is a registered trademark of The Reader's Digest Association, Inc.

LifeRich Publishing books may be ordered through booksellers or by contacting:

LifeRich Publishing
1663 Liberty Drive
Bloomington, IN 47403
www.liferichpublishing.com
844-686-9607

Because of the dynamic nature of the Internet, any web addresses or links contained in this book may have changed since publication and may no longer be valid. The views expressed in this work are solely those of the author and do not necessarily reflect the views of the publisher, and the publisher hereby disclaims any responsibility for them.

Any people depicted in stock imagery provided by Getty Images are models, and such images are being used for illustrative purposes only.
Certain stock imagery © Getty Images.

Scripture quotations marked NIV are taken from the Holy Bible, NEW INTERNATIONAL VERSION®, NIV® Copyright © 1973, 1978, 1984, 2011 by Biblica, Inc.® Used by permission. All rights reserved worldwide.

ISBN: 978-1-4897-4114-1 (sc)
ISBN: 978-1-4897-4113-4 (hc)
ISBN: 978-1-4897-4115-8 (e)

Printed in the United States of America

LifeRich Publishing rev. date: 07/26/2023

CONTENTS

GOD MADE THE WORLD
Genesis 1

The first day, God said, "Let there be light."
He called it day and then made the night.
We don't know how or understand why,
But on the second day, God created the sky.
The third day, God made the land and the seas,
Planting many beautiful plants and tall trees.
On the fourth day, God still was not done.
He put in the sky the stars, moon, and the sun.
God created all things in his own special way,
Making colorful birds and fish on the fifth day.
Animals came next, along with woman and man.
God finished on the sixth day, according to plan.
Finally, on the seventh day, God took a rest.
His creation was done, and it was the best.
The seventh day was made holy and blessed,
Reminding us to take one day a week to rest.

THE GARDEN OF EDEN
Genesis 2-3

God planted a garden and put Adam there. He
would work the ground and take care
Of the beautiful plants, flowers, and trees that
grew in the garden, in the cool breeze.
You can eat the fruit of all the trees but one. If you choose to
disobey, your life won't be fun. God carefully warned Adam, and
I'll tell you why. If Adam ate from this tree, he would die.
Not too many days passed, and it became known Adam needed a
helper, so he wouldn't be alone. God took a rib from Adam while
he was asleep and made from it a woman who was his to keep.
Along came a snake who was deceitful and sly. He questioned the
woman and told her a lie. "Is it true there is no tree in the garden
from which you can eat? You will never die or go down in defeat.
Your eyes will be opened, and you will now see
how good and evil affect you and me."
So the woman saw that the fruit was good to eat; she
ate it and shared with her husband the treat.
Immediately they realized things weren't the same. Recognizing their
sin, they were filled with shame. They became afraid of God and
wanted to hide, not wanting him to see their nakedness and pride.
Adam blamed the woman for causing him to sin. The snake deceived
the woman until she gave in. This is how we are tempted, causing
sin in our life. So always flee evil so it won't cause you strife.

God punished Adam and Eve and the snake, knowing the trouble and
pain that sin would make. Now having babies is painful and gardens
have weeds. And we all need God's forgiveness for our sinful deeds.

NOAH AND THE ARK
Genesis 6-8

God saw how the people were wicked and vain; it made him so
sad, his heart was filled with pain. He decided to make rain come
down from the sky, flooding the earth so everyone would die.
Noah and his family loved and feared the Lord; they walked close
to God, and him they adored. God chose Noah to build the ark, a
very big boat. "Carefully follow my instructions so it will float."
The ark was 450 feet long and 75 feet wide.
It had only one door that shut from the outside. There
were three floors, a total of forty-five feet tall,
Room for all the animals, both large and small.
It was time for the animals, at least two of each kind, to enter the ark.
Noah did not want any left behind. There were elephants and tigers. I can
imagine the fun, loading all the animals and birds on the ark one by one.
Finally, Noah and his family climbed aboard the big boat. It
began to rain, and after a few days, the ark started to float.
For forty days and forty nights, the heavy rain came down. It's
so sad that those who didn't follow God would drown.
The rain finally stopped, and God sent a strong breeze.
Noah couldn't wait for the day they could see the trees.
The water steadily went down until they firmly sat on the
east side of Turkey, in the mountains of Ararat.
Noah opened the window and sent a dove out to see if she could find a
place to make a nest in a tree. Seven days later, Noah sent her out again
to take a peek. This time she came back with an olive leaf in her beak.

God made a promise and put a rainbow in the sky, so every time we see
one, we will remember why God sent Jesus to die and pay for all our sin,
Giving us salvation if we only let him come in.

THE TOWER OF BABEL
Genesis 11:1–9

At one time, all the people of the earth spoke the same
language from childbirth. Some with a desire for power
came up with the idea to build a tall tower.
"Let's make some bricks and let them bake, and with
them the tower we will make. Building a city will give us a
great name and increase our own glory and fame."
The Lord came down to see their city and tower and decided to
take away some of their power. He mixed up their words so they
could not hear. Their speech was confused and very unclear.
Construction was stopped on their great city. The people didn't
follow God; what a great pity! Babel became the name of the
tall tower, one place where God took back his power.
What can we learn from this biblical story? Never be so proud
you can't give God the glory. Always follow the Lord, and
you will see the amazing ways he can use you and me!

ABRAHAM'S RESPONSE TO GOD
Genesis 22:1-14

God told Abraham to take Isaac, his son;
Abraham and Sarah had only one.
"Go to a mountain I will tell you about."
I am sure Abraham had a little bit of doubt.

"Sacrifice your son as a burnt offering to me."
God was testing Abraham to see,
Would he be obedient, and did he know
That faith is always the right way to go?

Early the next morning, Abraham was awake,
Preparing for the long journey he would take.
He cut enough wood for the sacrifice fire,
Loading everything the trip would require.

By faith and obedience, Abraham set out,
Trusting that God knew what this was about.
Abraham saw the mountain on the third day.
They took time to worship God and pray.

Isaac's responsibility was to carry the wood.
He never complained and obeyed, as he should.
He asked where the lamb was, and his father replied,
"You don't need to worry because God will provide."

9

Abraham tied up his son and put him on the wood,
About to do something he didn't know if he could.
With the knife ready, Abraham heard his name.
At just the right moment, an angel of God came.

"Don't do anything to Isaac; I know you fear me.
You can now untie your son and let him go free."
Abraham saw a male sheep caught by his horn.
He sacrificed the animal instead of his firstborn.

You can have faith when the going gets tough,
That God will provide and give you enough.
His grace and love will be just what you need.
Step out boldly by faith and allow God to lead.

JOSEPH
Genesis 37

Joseph was his father's most honored and loved son. His eleven brothers
hated him, and that was never fun. His father made a fancy-colored coat
for him to wear, just one more thing his brothers thought was not fair.
When Joseph was seventeen and a young man, he didn't know he was
a part of God's special plan. While taking care of the sheep, Joseph
had a dream. Telling his brothers was a mistake, it would seem.
In this dream they were all binding sheaves of grain. The sheaves bowed
to him, he would explain. "You really think that over us you will rule
or reign?" This dream made the brothers' anger much more plain.
To make matters worse, Joseph had a second dream; his father and
brothers all thought it was extreme. The sun, moon, and eleven stars to
him bowed down, making his brothers more jealous with an angry frown.
His brothers went with their sheep to another place. Joseph left to check
on them, hoping for their embrace. When they saw him coming, they
took his coat away and threw him in the bottom of an empty well to stay.
They sold him to a caravan that passed along their way, heading to Egypt
to sell their goods that day. What they did not know was that this was
in God's plan to bring salvation to his people in a way only God can.
Be prepared for the day when God chooses to use you. It may be
something special that he gives you to do. I am sure you are included in
God's perfect plan to bring salvation to some woman, child, or man.

MOSES
Exodus 2:1-10

The pharaoh of Egypt made an awful law: All
Jewish baby boys he wanted to kill
By drowning them in the river Nile,
Totally against their parents' will.
A couple from the house of Levi
Gave birth to a beautiful baby boy.
They hid him for three months,
Worried they would lose their joy.
When the baby could no longer be hid,
He was put in a basket covered with tar.
Placed in the reeds near the bank of the Nile,
watched by his sister from a place not far.
The pharaoh's daughter came to the river to bathe; she
saw the basket that was placed in the reeds.
When she opened it up and heard the baby cry, she
decided to take care of all of his needs.
The baby's sister asked if she could find someone
who could nurse and care for this little one.
Pharaoh's daughter agreed and offered to pay for this
Hebrew woman to care for her own son.
The child grew older, and the time came when he
Was the age to become part of Pharaoh's family.
He was named Moses for out of the water he came.
He would be the one God chose to set his people free.

MOSES AND THE BURNING BUSH
Exodus 3:1-4:17

While Moses was taking care of the sheep, the flock of Jethro, his father-
in-law, he came across a very strange sight; a burning bush is what he saw.
An angel of the Lord appeared to Moses in a
flaming bush that did not burn.
God called to him from within the bush, a
voice causing Moses's head to turn.
"Here I am," Moses said immediately to God.
"Take off your sandals, and stay where you are
For the place you are standing is holy ground.
I want to talk with you, so please don't go far.
I am the God of Abraham, Isaac, and Jacob; I am also your father's God."
When Moses heard this, he was afraid; he hid
his face because he was so awed.
"I see the pain and misery of my people; their
suffering is causing them to shout.
I want you to go to Pharaoh, king of Egypt, and
demand that he let them come out.
But Moses had several excuses,
Insisting he was not the right man to go.
"What if no one believes or listens to me? And
my speech is so awkward and slow."
Maybe you have felt the same way.
Maybe you are filled with fear.
Just remember that God made you
And has promised to always be near.

DAVID AND GOLIATH
1 Samuel 17

Goliath was a giant, standing over nine feet tall. One day he challenged
Israel to a serious brawl. "Choose a man to fight me," he shouted
and defied, not thinking of the living God he had just denied.
Saul and the Israelites were dismayed and terrified,
forgetting the power of their God in whom they relied.
Only seeing their problem, the enormity of their foe, they
cowered in his presence and did not want to go.
After forty days of defiance, David, son of Jesse, heard how
the giant rudely mocked God with every word. "No one
need lose heart because in God's power I will go. In God's
strength, I'll fight and conquer this mighty foe."
He carefully chose five stones from the nearby brook; in the name of the
Lord Almighty, his stance he took. And David with his sling aimed for
the giant's head. The stone hit its mark, and the enemy fell down dead.
There is an important lesson from this story today: When giants
threaten to defeat us along the way, do we forget the God we trust and
coil up in fear? Or do we trust his power, realizing he is always near?

ELIJAH CHALLENGES KING AHAB
1 Kings 18:16–40

Ahab, king of Israel, was a corrupt and evil man. Elijah was God's
prophet with a very special plan. Meet me on Mount Carmel so we
can clearly see who serves the true and living God on bended knee.
They cut a bull in pieces and laid it on some wood; the people all
agreed that this plan was very good. The living God would devour the
sacrifice by fire. This challenge would prove whose God was a liar.
The people called loudly to the name of their god, Baal. They soon
realized their frantic cries were to no avail. They shouted even louder, but
Baal failed to hear. That he would never answer became so very clear.
"Maybe he is sleeping or deep in thought," Elijah said.
"He might be traveling, on vacation; or could he be dead?
Maybe we should wake him up so that he can hear. We
would really like to know if he is alive and near."
Now it was Elijah's turn to demonstrate God's power. He
prayed to God, trusting the sacrifice he would devour. Twelve
big jars of water were poured on the meat and wood. While
all the people waited, around the altar they stood.
"Answer me today, O Lord, so all these people will know
you are God, and your mighty power will clearly show." Fire
came down, burning the sacrifice, water, and wood. Elijah's
God was real, now the people clearly understood.
When the people saw this, they fell on their faces and cried,
"The Lord, he is God," regretting they had ever denied. So
when you read this story, remember that God loves you,
wanting you to follow him down the only path that is true.

GOD PROVIDES FOR THE WIDOW
2 Kings 4:1-7

There was a woman whose husband had died. She needed help
and someone to be her guide. She could not pay her bills and had
very little food. What would she do? It had to affect her mood.
She talked to Elisha, a prophet of God, who listened even though
her story was a bit odd. Her creditor was coming to take her
boys away; she needed to find a way quickly, her debt to pay.
Elisha replied to the women, "How can I help you? Do
you have anything to give? Even a little will do."
"I have nothing in my house except a little oil. How
could that possibly relieve all this turmoil?"
"Go to your neighbors, and ask for an empty jar. Ask for as many
as you can, go near and go far. Go and fill each jar with oil, right
up to the top. When you have filled all the jars, the oil will stop.
Now go sell your oil so your debts you can pay. You can live on
the extra, so your boys can stay." So what can we learn from this
story today? God loves to provide and will show you the way.

NAAMAN HEALED OF LEPROSY
2 Kings 5:1–15

Once there was a very important man.
To be great in the army was his plan.
But things did not go as expected, you see.
Naaman became really sick with leprosy.
What should he do? Who would he go see?
Elisha, the man of God said, "Come and see me."
Naaman went to see what the prophet would say.
"Go wash yourself seven times in the Jordan today."
The words made Naaman mad, and he would not obey,
Thinking he could be healed in a more respectable way.
"Just wave your hand over the spot, and call on the Lord.
I should not have to wash in a dirty river to be restored."
After talking to his servants, Naaman decided to go
And wash seven times in the Jordan River's flow.
In simple obedience, Naaman did what he was told.
God instantly healed him, an amazing thing to behold.
Whatever God asks you to do, it is important to obey.
Immediately humble yourself, and do it God's way,
And you, like Naaman, will clearly know and see
There is only one true God, and he is definitely for me.

DANIEL'S RESOLVE
Daniel 1

Daniel resolved not to defile himself with royal food and wine
given to him by King Nebuchadnezzar; yes, he decided to decline.
Several young men had been chosen to help serve the king, ones
who were handsome and capable of learning anything.
Shadrach, Meshach, and Abednego joined Daniel to be trained. For
three years, all the ways of the Babylonians were explained. When
the four asked permission to not eat the royal food and drink, their
chief official was worried about what the king would think.
"Please test your servants with only vegetables and water to drink. After
ten days, compare us with the others, and tell us what you think." In
ten days, they looked healthier and better nourished than the rest;
God graciously blessed their resolve and helped them pass the test.
God gave them knowledge and understanding, blessing their minds,
so they could understand literature, visions, and dreams of all kinds.
At the end of their rigorous training, the king was pleased to find,
them ten times more fit than any other, both in body and in mind.
Are we committed to stand for truth and follow God's perfect way.
Or will we fall when we face temptation, immediately going astray?
Let's resolve not to defile our lives with the sin we see on every side.
Depending on God's resurrection power, let Jesus be our guide.

THE FIERY FURNACE
Daniel 3

King Nebuchadnezzar made a huge image of gold. At ninety feet tall, it
was quite a sight to behold. He ordered all the people to worship and
fall down. The threat of the blazing furnace made everyone frown.
The instruments and music created quite the sound. Immediately, all the
people fell to the ground. Except for Shadrach, Meshach, and Abednego,
the Jews who were not afraid of the king; God they would choose.
The three Jews were summoned before the angry king. A second chance
was given to forget this whole thing. "Worship my image, or to the fiery
furnace you will go. You will regret disobeying me and becoming my foe."
Shadrach and his two friends replied to the king, "The God we serve is
able to save us from anything. And even if he chooses to not rescue us
from the flame, we won't worship your gods and bring ourselves shame."
The king was now furious; his attitude changed. Heating
the furnace seven times hotter, he easily arranged. The
three were bound and thrown into the blazing fire. How
could the results be anything but incredibly dire?
When the king looked into the furnace, he was alarmed.
There were four men, not three, unbound and unharmed.
Seeing that their God had saved them, he began to shout,
"Servants of the Most High God, I want you to come out."
Shadrach and friends came out of the fire feeling well.
Their robes were not scorched and not even a smell. The
hair on their heads was not singed, not even a burn, a
clear miracle from God. What lessons can we learn?

When faced with big problems with the need to be brave, will we trust
the one and only God who can save? Like King Nebuchadnezzar, whose
heart God changed, let him perform the miracles he has already arranged.

DANIEL AND THE LION'S DEN
Daniel 6

Daniel was one of the top three administrators in the land,
so qualified, the king planned to put him first in command.
The other leaders tried to figure out how to bring him down;
they wanted in the worst way to wear the leader's crown.
They could not find fault with Daniel's character or work; he
was trustworthy and his responsibilities would not shirk. They
changed their course of action toward this godly man. To trip
him up in prayer or worship now became their plan.
King Darius was encouraged to make an edict and then
agreed to throw all who disobeyed it into the lion's den. So
eagerly, all they had to do was wait patiently and see, knowing
Daniel would keep praying to his God faithfully.
When Daniel learned about the law, a decision soon he made;
he would kneel by the window, where he had always prayed. He
gave thanks to God, asking him for help three times a day. No
matter what the outcome, faithful to God he would stay.
Daniel's enemies reported to the king what they had seen,
that Daniel continued praying as was his daily routine. The
king was distressed to the point he could not sleep, wishing
he had not made the law that now he had to keep.
Daniel was thrown in with the lions, and early the next day,
the king with an anguished voice checked without delay. "Did
the God you serve continually rescue you last night?"
"God sent an angel to shut the lion's mouth, and I'm all right."
The king was overjoyed to see Daniel still alive and then
ordered the accusers and their families into the lion's den.
They were crushed before they hit the ground so all could see
there is always great blessing in following God faithfully.

JONAH AND THE GREAT FISH
Jonah 1-3

There was a man name Jonah that God told to go,
Travel to Nineveh and preach but he told God no.
Jonah ran away from the Lord and went the other way,
Why he tried to go to Tarshish, the Bible doesn't say.

In Joppa, Jonah found a ship and gladly paid the fare,
He was running from the Lord and really didn't care.
A violent storm arose and threatened to sink the ship,
The sailors were afraid for their lives, what a scary trip.

Call upon your God so that we don't sink and die,
The sea got even rougher and they all wondered why.
Finally, Jonah told them to throw him into the sea,
I know that this violent storm is here because of me.

When they threw Jonah overboard, the sea grew still,
God prepared a great fish to swallow him like a pill.
After three days, lots of prayer and at God's command,
The big fish vomited Jonah up onto dry land.

God told Jonah a second time to pack up and go,
And warn sinful Nineveh with a message of woe.
This time Jonah obeyed the word of the Lord and went,
Delivering words of judgment with which he was sent.

The Ninevites believed God and prepared a fast,
Where they asked forgiveness for their sins at last.
When God saw the change in their heart,
He forgave their sin and gave them a new start.

So what can we learn from this Bible story today?
It's always important to love God and obey.
Never run away from the Lord. He wants you to stay,
He will keep your heart tender as you walk in his way.